Marked by Love
The Call to Love God, the Community, and Other Christians
Floyd Gary Pierce

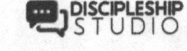

Discipleship Studio

To the loving people of White Plains Baptist Church in Scottsville, Kentucky. It is a joy to serve as your Pastor.

Marked By Love : The Call to Love God, the Community, and Other Christians

Copyright © 2023 by Floyd Gary Pierce.
For more, visit floydgarypierce.com.

Paperback ISBN: 978-1-965044-00-1
Audiobook ISBN: 978-1-965044-04-9
eBook ISBN: 978-1-965044-01-8

Requests for information should be addressed to:
Discipleship Studio, 186 Woodbrier Dr, Scottsville, Kentucky 42164

Introduction

Love God, the Community, and Other Christians

As a Christian, Jesus calls you to love God and your neighbor. Jesus says in Matthew, "And he said to him, 'You shall love the Lord your God with all your heart and with all your soul and with all your mind. This is the great and first commandment. And a second is like it: You shall love your neighbor as yourself.'" (Matthew 22:37-39, ESV).

Love God, the community, and other Christians. In *Marked By Love: The Call to Love God, the Community, and Other Christians*, I outline a few simple spiritual disciplines for you to practice expressing love to God. Loving God is the most important thing you can do as a Christian.

In this book, I also segment your neighbor into two groups who you are called to love. Love your lost neighbors in the community you live in, which really extends to the entire world. Love your neighbor in your church. There are dozens of "one another" passages that speak to those who share your faith, specifically those in your church. Love other Christians outside your church, also, but understand there is a special connection to those you fellowship with regularly. You are called to love your fellow church members. That is the focus of the "one another" passages in the New Testament.

The last chapter focuses on loving kids. Jesus loves kids. Because of that, you are called to love kids, too, for the sake of the Gospel.

Contents

Contents

Chapter One
A Loving Christian

Love is essential for the Christian. Love is a bedrock belief in Christianity. God loves you and in response, you are to love Him and others. If you aren't a loving Christian, you should be concerned if you have Christ at all. John writes, "Anyone who does not love does not know God, because God is love." (1 John 4:8 [English Standard Version]).

"God is love." You have probably heard that phrase. It's found here in 1 John 4:8. This phrase does more than just describe God. John wrote it to explain why Christians should love. God is more than love. However, He is love. Because He is love, you should love. Love is such an important aspect of God that those who follow Him must have it too. We must love. You and I must love. It is not optional. To follow Jesus means you must love. You must be a loving Christian.

Define love. As you think about how you would define love, many ideas will come to mind. God calls

Christians to love, but it is difficult to know how to love and be obedient to this command. Language limits your understanding of love. Opinions cloud your application of love. Experiences can shape your expression of love.

Language of Love

The English language poorly defines love. There is one word for love in English. "I love pizza," and "I love my wife" use the same word, but "love" means different things (hopefully) in these two statements. I enjoy pizza. Pizza is one of my favorite foods to eat. In fact, I have a shirt that says, "I wonder if pizza thinks of me, too." It is an accurate statement to say in English, "I love pizza."

I love my wife. I feel and act differently toward my wife than I do with my slice of pizza, but English limits me to this same word. This is bound to create problems for you as you attempt to follow God's command to love. Should you "pizza love" others or should you "wife love" others? Perhaps it is something entirely different. I will discuss the language difficulty later in this chapter.

Opinions of Love

Even if you could easily define love, you probably know people who have different opinions of love. You might hear people say something like, "For me, love is..." and then someone else who disagrees would say, "Well, for me, love is..." Everybody has an opinion about love and how to express, respond, or act upon it.

For most, love isn't like math, where there's only one right answer to 2 + 2. Love has many definitions. Even if you can get the language right, there are countless opinions on how to live out love.

Experiences of Love

Experiences shape opinions. You may know of people who have experienced abuse in the name of love. Others manipulated, and it has been called love. Still, others have had nurturing experiences with love. There are as many experiences of love as there are opinions of love. Add this to the difficulty in the language, and the limitless opinions about love, and you have an almost impossible task of understanding what God wants from you regarding love. So what are you to do?

Let me shift for just a moment. You have a purpose in life. God has a reason for you to exist right now where you live. You have a God-given purpose. Rick Warren starts his devotional book, *Purpose Driven Life*, with this:

> "The purpose of your life is far greater than your own personal fulfillment, your peace of mind, or even your happiness. It's far greater than your family, your career, or even your wildest dreams and ambitions. If you want to know why you were placed on this planet, you must begin with God. You were born by his purpose and for his purpose." - Rick Warren, Purpose Driven Life.[1]

Your purpose is to serve God and His will. He is your Creator, Savior, and Lord. God tells you in the Bible how you are to serve Him. If you are a Christian, you must be a person of the Bible. Spend time with your

---

1. Rick Warren, The Purpose Driven Life: What on Earth Am I Here For? (Grand Rapids, MI: Zondervan, 2012).

Bible and read it, learn it, and apply it to your life and your world. Allow the Bible to shape your worldview.

The Bible speaks of love. In fact, the New Testament speaks often about the ideas and actions associated with love. Below I list how many times each book in the New Testament speaks of love. I found this eye-opening. I think you will, too.

Love in the New Testament

Matthew – 13

Mark – 5

Luke – 18

John – 57

Romans – 17

1 Corinthians – 17

2 Corinthians – 13

Galatians – 5

Ephesians – 20

Philippians – 6

Colossians – 5

1 Thessalonians – 8

2 Thessalonians – 4

1 Timothy – 6

2 Timothy – 7

Titus – 4

Philemon – 3

Hebrews – 6

James – 3

1 Peter – 9

2 Peter – 2

1 John – 46

2 John – 4

3 John – 2

Jude – 3

Revelation – 7

Christians Should Love Well

Because the New Testament speaks of it so much, Christians should love well. You should know what it means to love and how to actively live out love.

Look at that chart again. John speaks 116 times about love in his writings. Paul speaks 115 times about it in his writings. Love is in every book of the New Testament, except for Acts.

Love is something Christians should know and do well, but sometimes Christians mess it up.

Some Christians really struggle with the thoughts and actions of love. Do you? The struggle stems from the language difficulty of love. Christians listen to the world's definition of love and incorrectly apply it to Christian love. It's not the same. In fact, it is far from the same.

The Baker Encyclopedia of the Bible helps us understand the difficulty of the idea of love.

> **Love:** The first and last word in Christian theology and ethics. It is therefore important to understand clearly this exceedingly ambiguous term.[2]

Wouldn't you agree that love is one of the hardest definitions to agree upon? If you took a quick survey at your workplace, I am positive that you would get different definitions of love. In the world's attempt to seek acceptance for whatever people want to do, the world has come up with phrases and definitions like, "Love is love."

Grammatically, what does that mean?

It means nothing. One of the first things you learn in English class is that you can't use the word in

---

2. R.E.O. White, "Love," Baker Encyclopedia of the Bible (Grand Rapids, MI: Baker Book House, 1988), 1357.

its definition, right? So with a definition of love like this, it means nothing.

When a word means nothing, then it can mean anything.

Aren't you seeing that today? The world outside the church is telling themselves and those inside the church that love means anything you want it to mean. The world has done this with the definition of "truth." Now the term "truth" is meaningless. People speak of "my truth" and "your truth."

When a word means nothing, it can mean anything. Words and definitions matter. The lost definition of love is affecting the church. It is probably affecting you, too.

Do you follow the world's definition of love? Are you making up your own definition, or are you using the Bible to define love in your relationships in the church and in the community?

I want to draw your attention to one of the most popular passages of Scripture defining love, 1 Corinthians 13. You have likely heard it read at a wedding you've attended. Let's look at the entire chapter and allow the Bible to define love.

If I speak in the tongues of men and of angels, but have not love, I am a noisy gong or a clanging cymbal. And if I have prophetic powers, and understand all mysteries and all knowledge, and if I have all faith, so as to remove mountains, but have not love, I am nothing. If I give away all I have, and if I deliver up my body to be burned, but have not love, I gain nothing. Love is patient and kind; love does not envy or boast; it is not arrogant or rude. It does not insist on its own way; it is not irritable or resentful; it does not rejoice at wrongdoing, but rejoices with the truth. Love bears all things, believes all things, hopes all things, endures all things. Love never ends. As for prophecies, they will pass away; as for tongues, they will cease; as for knowledge, it will pass away. For we know in part and we prophesy in part, but when the perfect comes, the partial will pass away. When I was a child, I spoke like a child, I thought like a child, I reasoned like a child. When I became a man, I gave up childish ways. For now we see in a mirror dimly, but then face to face. Now I know in part; then I shall know fully, even as I have been fully known. So now faith, hope, and love abide, these three; but the greatest of these is love. (1 Corinthians 13:1-13.)

Allow the Bible to Define the Words it Defines

There is a clear definition of love right here in Chapter 13, isn't there? Do you see it?

As a point of historical context, many believe that Paul wrote what you have in Chapter 13 separately before he wrote the first letter to the Corinthian church. He then inserted it into his letter to the church because it applied to what they were struggling with. It has nothing to do with romantic love, but how the church should act on love within itself.

There are several types of "love" found in the Bible. There are several words in Greek that define love's actions and objects. English uses only one word. The phrase "love is love" attempts to define acceptance of sinful romantic love. The Greek word for romantic love is eros. Eros does not appear in the New Testament.

The Greek word that we have throughout 1 Corinthians 13 is agape. Agape is the word for love most commonly used in the New Testament.

The Greek language has a couple of other words for love besides eros and agape. Phileo is brotherly affection for someone. It is very similar to agape, but without divine inclusion. Similarly, the term for familiar love is storge. It is the type of warm friendship the world has outside of God.

In English, the word is love for all of these terms. It is easy to misuse, misapply, and misunderstand what you mean when you say, "love."

It is very easy for people to take the phrase "love is love" and misapply it to mean eros is agape. Eros doesn't mean agape. Without understanding the Greek language, it is very easy to misunderstand love.

Also, if teenagers are anything like they used to be when I was one, guys often misunderstand agape or phileo and think it means eros. When a girl is kind to a guy, it doesn't necessarily mean she likes him. Have you ever had that misunderstanding in your teen years? I sure did.

Let's define agape.

Agape: The Greek term for divine love as opposed to worldly love, it can be directed towards God, Christ or fellow Christians.[3]

This divine love is what you have throughout 1 Corinthians 13. As you love God, and other Christians, this divine love is what you think and act upon. This word, agape, is the love that you show to the community around you, too. Agape is a gospel-focused love.

Importance of Love

So why is love, divine love, agape, so important for Christians? Look back at 1 Corinthians 13:1-3.

If I speak in the tongues of men and of angels, but have not love, I am a noisy gong or a clanging cymbal. And if I have prophetic powers, and understand all

---

3. Ron Geaves, "Agape," in Continuum Glossary of Religious Terms (London; New York: Continuum, 2022), 9.

mysteries and all knowledge, and if I
have all faith, so as to remove mountains, but have not love, I am nothing. If
I give away all I have, and if I deliver up
my body to be burned, but have not love,
I gain nothing. (1 Corinthians 13:1-3.)

Here you see the importance of Christian love. Paul
is writing this to the Corinthian church because
some are bragging about having certain spiritual
gifts and those gifts being better than others. Paul
corrects the church here by saying that love (agape)
is the most important gift. He then defines what
love (agape) is and does. Paul closes the passage
reminding the church that love (agape) is the most
important gift.

Be a loving Christian. For the sake of the gospel and
others, you must love well and always.

Why? Paul tells you.

The first thing Paul addresses is speaking in
tongues. This is a point of pride for some. Paul
doesn't say not to speak in tongues. He doesn't deny
the benefit to the person or the church, but he says
that if you practice speaking in tongues without

love, no one will listen to you. You will come across as an unpleasantly loud noise.

I don't practice speaking in tongues. I believe this gift has ceased, so what does this passage mean for me? You may believe differently about tongues than I do. We can still be friends. This is an issue that is open for dialogue. Regardless of whatever you believe about tongues, we speak. You and I speak. You speak to church members, those in the community, and your family.

You speak. As you speak, speak the gospel. Speak the truth. But you must not only speak the truth. The gospel and truth can be offensive, especially as you confront sin. How are you to speak the truth that can be offensive?

With love.

Paul addresses another church with this same idea. It must have been a problem for people in the early church. It shouldn't surprise you that it is a problem for the church today. In Ephesians, Paul says, "Rather, speaking the truth in love, we are to grow up in every way into him who is the head, into Christ." (Ephesians 4:15.)

Speak the truth.

You must speak the truth.

If you don't speak the truth, you allow sin to run rampant in your church and in your community. If you don't speak the truth, people will be blinded by their own sins. Without Christ, they will spend an eternity being punished for their sins.

You miss the mark when you only speak the truth. Speak the truth with love. If you don't have love in your truth-speaking, you become annoying, and people will ignore you. No one will listen. Speak in a way that people will listen. Speak the truth with love.

Paul tells you in 1 Corinthians 13 that if you teach, or if you have the gifts of wisdom, knowledge, and faith, but you do so without love, it's meaningless. Without love, your teaching, your wisdom, your knowledge, and even your faith are nothing. Love is supremely important.

Paul also shows you here that if you sacrifice, even to the point of giving away everything you have, including your very life, without love, you gain nothing. There is no reward for your sacrifices without love being part of that sacrifice. Love is of ultimate importance.

Defining Love

So let's now set out to define love with the Bible. The Bible defines love. When the Bible defines words, use that definition as a Christian. There is no other option for a follower of Jesus.

You can't let the world around you inform the definition of a word that the Bible defines for you. It is part of dying to the world and following Jesus. Even if you don't like the definition. Even if your family members, friends, or co-workers don't like the definition the Bible gives you, you must let the Bible define the words for you it defines.

The world doesn't like the Bible's definition of love. But that should be expected, right? It's not surprising when those who don't follow Jesus disagree and even hate what the Bible says.

Be careful not to allow their hatred and disagreement to affect your love for the Bible. As a Christian, you follow Jesus. As you follow Jesus, love His Word.

Let's look back at 1 Corinthians here to get our definition of love.

Love is patient and kind; love does not
envy or boast; it is not arrogant or rude.
It does not insist on its own way; it is
not irritable or resentful; it does not rejoice at wrongdoing, but rejoices with
the truth. Love bears all things, believes
all things, hopes all things, endures all
things. Love never ends. (1 Corinthians
13:4-8.)

This is beautifully poetic, isn't it? Don't get lost in its
beauty and miss its meaning. The Bible defines love.
What does it say?

Love is Patient and Kind

Paul defines love with very difficult actions: patience and kindness. These are hard, right? For
many, patience is extremely difficult. It is for me. I
usually know when I am being impatient. The horn
honks, there are verbal reminders of the time, a
relational distance appears, and so on. You probably
know when you are being impatient, too.

Kindness is much harder for us. You live in a world
that is unkind. The world celebrates unkindness.
Babies quickly express unkindness and it remains to
old age.

In the world of sports, kindness is not something a coach puts on his or her resume. Have you ever seen a video of a coach showing kindness to a referee who makes an obviously terrible call? You normally see him screaming in his face, don't you?

Much like impatience, unkindness is everywhere. Unkindness can mask itself behind humor and sarcasm. Unkind words are often spoken in humor or sarcasm, so that when the truth is discovered, the unkind person can quickly dismiss it as a joke or as if they didn't really mean it. This is probably in your home. It's in the schools. It's in your church.

It should not be.

Love is patient and kind. Love considers how a person's words and actions will be received before saying or doing them. Love is hard, but it is what God wants from you.

Love Does Not Envy or Boast

Someone who loves doesn't think too highly of themself or isn't upset when someone else succeeds. Love looks to celebrate others and minimize themself. When your company overlooks you and promotes someone else, love does not envy. When people celebrate you for a job well done, love doesn't boast. Love is hard, but it is what God wants from you.

Love is Not Arrogant or Rude

Arrogance and rudeness have no place in the life of a Christian. They have no place in the life of a pastor or deacon. They have no place in the life of any person who claims to follow Jesus. Love is not arrogant or rude. In arrogance, people think too highly of themselves. In rudeness, people place their needs before others. Christians put others before themselves, for the sake of the gospel. You love because He first loved you. God met your needs in Christ. Remove arrogance and rudeness from inside the walls of your church. Love should be in the air of your church and within your circles of relationship. Love is hard, but it is what God wants from you.

Love Does Not Insist on its Own Way

Love puts the needs of others before your own. It doesn't demand its own way. It recognizes the temptation and sin that can follow someone who has to have their way all the time. Do you know people who always insist on their way? It's their way or the highway. This is not loving. Love considers those around them and allows others to have input. It looks to others' needs and seeks to meet them. Love is hard, but it is what God wants from you.

Love is Not Irritable or Resentful

Love isn't grumpy. It doesn't hold a grudge. Love doesn't keep a record of wrongs. A loving Christian has a cheerful spirit about them. There is joy in their life that others see. There might be a history of hurt, but it doesn't affect their current and future joyfulness. Choosing to love others involves choosing joy over past hurt. Choosing to love others involves forgiving other's past sins against you. Love is hard, but it is what God wants from you.

Love Does Not Rejoice at Wrongdoing, but Rejoices with the Truth

This is where the world will attack the Bible's definition of love. This is where you are tempted to bend the rules of a biblical definition of love. The world doesn't recognize truth and doesn't believe it's wrong to sin.

You live in a world where individuals want others to accept and rejoice in their decisions, whether they be wrong or right. Love doesn't rejoice in ANY sin.

It doesn't accept the sinful decisions of others as okay. Love rejoices when the wrongdoer turns to the truth found in the Bible and repents. Love is hard, but it is what God wants from you.

Love Bears All Things, Hopes All Things, and Endures All Things

Love is hard. It really is. When you love someone, you put up with a lot of junk, but you do so patiently because you trust God will work in the lives of those you love. I don't mean just their initial response to the gospel. It is much more than that. Paul wrote this passage to a church in 1 Corinthians 13. He is instructing them how to love each other even after salvation.

Sin continues in the believer even after salvation. As you love others, you put up with a lot of stuff. You trust God to do what He does, which is change lives from the inside out. Love puts up with a lot, and trusts that God will work, but love also endures. It sticks around. With wisdom, remain with those you love. (If you find yourself in an abusive situation, talk to others around you to seek wisdom on how to express love. Don't remain in an abusive situation.

Love from a distance, at least for a while.) Love is hard, but it is what God wants from you.

Love Never Ends

Love lasts forever. You will continue to love for all eternity. You will love well in the next life, but God doesn't want you to wait until then. Christian love never ends. It begins when you follow Jesus.

Love seeks the best for someone else.

This definition takes all that 1 Corinthians gives you and puts it into an easily memorable sentence. Love seeks the best for someone else. As you love, seek the best for someone else. You are patient and kind; you do not envy or boast; you are not arrogant or rude; you don't insist on your own way; you are not irritable or resentful; you do not rejoice at sin and wrongdoing, but you rejoice with them as they turn from sin and believe the truth that is found the Bible. You bear, hope, and endure all things with others. This is a biblical definition of love.

If you can't remember all of 1 Corinthians 13 as your definition of love, you can probably remember 1 Corinthians 10:24 as your definition of love.

"Let no one seek his own good, but the good of his neighbor." (1 Corinthians 10:24.)

This is love: seeking the best for someone else.

Chapter Two

Loving God

Why love God? Does God need people to love Him? Does God want people to love Him?

> And I said, "O LORD God of heaven, the great and awesome God who keeps covenant and steadfast love with those who love him and keep his command- ments." (Nehemiah 1:5.)

God is faithful and loves you. God showers you with His love as you love and obey Him. One of God's defining characteristics is that God is love. We read about this in 1 John in the last chapter.

> Whoever confesses that Jesus is the Son of God, God abides in him, and he in God. So we have come to know and to believe the love that God has for us.

God is love, and whoever abides in love
abides in God, and God abides in him. (1
John 4:15-16.)

If you believe and confess that Jesus is God, the Son,
then love God because God is love. God's love is in
you as you express love toward Him. Loving God and
following Jesus go hand in hand.

In this the love of God was made man-
ifest among us, that God sent his only
Son into the world, so that we might live
through him. In this is love, not that we
have loved God but that he loved us and
sent his Son to be the propitiation for
our sins. (1 John 4:9-10.)

John echoed this sentiment in his gospel account.

For God so loved the world, that he gave
his only Son, that whoever believes in
him should not perish but have eternal
life. (John 3:16.)

Jesus is speaking to Nicodemus, a religious leader of the Jews. As a Jew, and even more so as a Pharisee, Nicodemus desired to love and serve God. He tried to do that by following the Law in the Old Testament. Nicodemus knew the Law and loved the Law. He recognized something in Jesus that he couldn't quite figure out, and thought it worth exploring. Jesus was proving Himself to be the Son of God, and Nicodemus noticed. He approached Jesus with several questions. Jesus said to him that people must be born again before they can see the Kingdom of God. You must, through faith and by God's grace, become a new creation. You must be born again if you are to experience God's ideal for your life and the world around you. This is what Jesus tells Nicodemus. Then Jesus explains that, and it is in this context, we have the most widely known verse in the Bible, John 3:16.

Love God Because He First Loved You

John 3:16 is great, but there is much more right after it. Here is the complete paragraph following John 3:16.

> For God so loved the world, that he gave
> his only Son, that whoever believes in

him should not perish but have eternal
life. For God did not send his Son into
the world to condemn the world, but
in order that the world might be saved
through him. Whoever believes in him
is not condemned, but whoever does
not believe is condemned already, because he has not believed in the name
of the only Son of God. And this is
the judgment: the light has come into
the world, and people loved the dark-
ness rather than the light because their
works were evil. For everyone who does
wicked things hates the light and does
not come to the light, lest his works
should be exposed. But whoever does
what is true comes to the light, so that it
may be clearly seen that his works have
been carried out in God. (John 3:16-21.)

Love God because He first loved you. As you love
God, you prove to others that you belong to Him.
Your love for God shows His love for you and others.
Those who aren't following Jesus can't and won't
love God correctly because they haven't accepted
God's love for them.

Love for God begins with accepting God's love for you. God loves you and sent Jesus to redeem you. The right response is love for God. Accept God's love and love Him back.

Have you ever battled cancer or known someone who has? So much uncertainty lies beyond that initial diagnosis. But if you meet with your doctor and she follows a treatment path that successfully cures the cancer, you would think your doctor is the best. You would tell others how your doctor worked to beat the terrible thing that was affecting your body. You would have an affection for that doctor, medical team, and the facility because you realized that without their intervention, you would have died. The cancer would have destroyed you.

It's the same with sin, but on a much bigger scale.

If you have cancer and don't know it, do you still have cancer?

Yes.

If you have cancer and do not know it, will cancer still affect the body the same way if you knew about it?

Yes, of course.

It is usually because the body is being affected by cancer that people seek medical help. It's when someone realizes something is wrong that they seek to understand it with hopes to correct it.

Cancer is awful. It's terrible. Cancer can take life. But there is something much worse than cancer. There is something that can take much more than your life.

Sin is worse than cancer. It can take your life and soul forever. Sin is in you right now. Apart from Christ, sin will take your life, soul, joy, and everything forever. Much more powerful than a doctor or medical treatment, you have Jesus to take your sin away from you, to give you life everlasting.

You are dead in your sin and destined for an eternity separated from everything you love and find joy in, but God shows you His love for you and gives you Jesus to take away that sin. He brings you to a spiritually healthy place for eternity. Accept that and respond with love for God.

Love God Because He Commands You

Loving God should be a natural response, but humans are forgetful. In His loving kindness to you, God commands you to love Him. He does this in

many places, including in the Ten Commandments
and, in Jesus' words in Matthew 22, the Greatest
Commandment.

> You shall love the Lord your God
> with all your heart and with all your
> soul and with all your mind. This
> is the great and first commandment.
> (Matthew 22:37-38.)

Jesus commands you to love God with all your heart,
soul, and mind. Did you know that when Jesus was
saying this, He was quoting Scripture?

Right here, as Jesus lays out the Greatest Commandment, He is quoting the Old Testament, almost
word for word.

> You shall love the LORD your God with
> all your heart and with all your soul and
> with all your might. (Deuteronomy 6:5.)

Isn't it interesting that Jesus quotes the Old Testament? When you see the Old Testament quoted, it
is important to recognize it. Many people think the
Old Testament is outdated or not applicable any-

more. But the truth is, the Old Testament is often quoted in the New Testament. There are around 300 quotations from the Old Testament in the New Testament. The New Testament isn't completely new or different from the Old Testament.

How to Love God

So how can you love God? How can you express love to God? You cannot do it outside of Jesus. If you want to love God, you must do so by faith in Jesus. In the Old Testament, Habakkuk 2:4 helps us understand this.

> The righteous shall live by his faith.
> (Habakkuk 2:4.)

Paul quotes this passage in Romans 1:17 and Galatians 3:11. The author of Hebrews quotes it in 10:38, and John uses this idea to frame his thoughts in John 3:36. You love God out of your faith in Him. This translates to every aspect of your life. The righteous live by faith.

Hebrews 11-12 is a great section of Scripture for you to explore to understand this idea of loving God out of your faith in Him. Hebrews 11:6 helps you

understand your expression of love for God coming
from your faith.

> And without faith it is impossible to
> please him, for whoever would draw
> near to God must believe that he ex-
> ists and that he rewards those who seek
> him. (Hebrews 11:6.)

You must have faith to even please God. Outside of
faith in God, you displease God. If you recognize you
don't believe that God exists, you are displeasing
God. It is impossible for you to please God.

Maybe you're not an atheist, someone who believes
there is no God. Perhaps you are agnostic, someone
who believes there is a God, but He is unknowable.
It is impossible to please God without faith. Without
faith, you cannot love God. Without faith, you are an
enemy of God, and your sin will cause you to reap
the eternal punishment of your sin.

Let me repeat John 3:16 here, "For God so loved
the world, that he gave his only Son, that whoever
believes in him should not perish but have eternal
life."

This is the faith that pleases God. This is the faith that we express our love for God with. Faith is active. It's not just a mental acknowledgment. It's not a passive belief in something.

God uses faith to save you. It redeems you. It rescues you. Faith completes you.

But faith is expressed through works.

This is a biblical idea coming from the Old Testament that is repeated in the New Testament. In Genesis 15, you have God's covenant with Abram. This is before his name changed to Abraham. I won't recount the whole narrative here, but God makes promises to Abram.

> And he believed the LORD, and he counted it to him as righteousness. And he said to him, "I am the LORD who brought you out from Ur of the Chaldeans to give you this land to possess." But he said, "O Lord GOD, how am I to know that I shall possess it?" He said to him, "Bring me a heifer three years old, a female goat three years old, a ram three years old, a turtledove, and a young pigeon." And he brought

him all these, cut them in half, and laid
each half over against the other. But he
did not cut the birds in half. (Genesis
15:6-10.)

Abram's faith made him righteous, but works quickly
followed it. Abram's works displayed his faith. Paul
quotes parts of this passage in Romans 4. James
quotes this narrative in James 2 as he rightly says
faith without works is dead.

But someone will say, "You have faith
and I have works." Show me your faith
apart from your works, and I will show
you my faith by my works. You believe
that God is one; you do well. Even the
demons believe—and shudder! (James
2:18-19.)

James is saying that faith, apart from works, is the
same type of faith that demons have, but they shudder in that belief.

Martin Luther, the Reformer, says it this way: "We
are saved by faith alone, but the faith that saves is
never alone."

Works follow faith. You love God by your works that flow from your faith. Note that I didn't say you love God with your works alone, but with your works that flow from your faith.

Spiritual Disciplines Help You Love God

I want to point you to three types of spiritual disciplines you can practice regularly as you express your love to God. The full list is much longer. These three disciplines should always be a part of the life of a Christian expressing love to God. I will pull these ideas from "Spiritual Disciplines for the Christian Life" by Donald Whitney. This is an excellent book to help you grow in your faith.

Bible Intake

Love God by interacting with the Bible. The Bible is God's Word to you. Spend time with it as you show love to God. The following list is from Dr. Whitney's book.

Six Ways of Interacting with Scripture

- Hearing God's Word
- Reading God's Word

- Studying God's Word

- Memorizing God's Word

- Meditating on God's Word

- Applying God's Word

Dr. Whitney says that hearing God's Word is the easiest of the disciplines. This is easily accomplished be regularly attending a church that preaches the Bible.

When it comes to reading the Bible, Dr. Whitney gives an alarming statistic in his book. He says that around 23% of professing Christians never read the Bible.[1] About 1 in 4 people who claim Christ as their Lord and Savior never read His Words to us. Let that not be true of you. To love God is to read His Words to you. Spend time in Scripture. Because you recognize the closeness that it brings to you and God. Wouldn't you agree that if spending time with God in His Word brings you closer to Him, that time away from Him and His Word creates a relational separation from Him?

---

1. Donald S. Whitney, Spiritual Disciplines for the Christian Life (Colorado Springs, CO: NavPress, 1991), 32.

Are you spiritually frustrated or indifferent? Do you pull away from God-honoring thoughts and activities? Are you beginning to question things you have always believed about God? Are you spending time with God reading His Words to you? If you are not reading the Bible and have negative feelings toward God-honoring things, then spend time with God in His Word. Let the truth you confess in the Bible draw you back to God.

As you get into the habit of reading the Bible regularly, you can then move on to studying it, memorizing it, meditating on it, and applying it. But these latter ones can't be accomplished if you are not reading the Bible regularly. The first way you love God is by spending time with Him interacting with the Bible.

Prayer

As you regularly interact with Scripture, you continue to show love to God by prayer. The Bible is full of commands to pray. If you aren't praying regularly, you are being disobedient.

> Continue steadfastly in prayer, being
> watchful in it with thanksgiving. (Colos-
> sians 4:2.)

> Pray without ceasing. (1 Thessalonians
> 5:17.)

Love God by praying to Him. He hears your prayers. God acts upon your prayers. He answers your prayers. You have direct access to the Creator and Sustainer of the universe through your prayers. Pray to Him.

Devote yourself to continual prayer.

As a follower of Jesus, show love to God by praying without ceasing. Dr. Whitney says that you learn to pray. For many people, praying is an arduous task. Don't let that keep you from praying; learn to pray. You can learn to pray in four different ways.

Learning to Pray

- by Praying, Using Matthew 6 as a Guide

- by Thinking Deeply (Meditating) on the Bible

- by Praying with Others

- by Reading about Prayer

Worship

As you spend personal time with God interacting with the Bible, worship should follow. As you uncover the truth that is found in God's Word, and as you approach Him in prayer, worship Him. Worship is expressing to God His worth. Think of it as worth-ship.

Dr. Whitney describes it this way in his book, "To worship God in spirit is to worship from the inside out, and we are to worship according to the truth of Scripture. We worship God as He is revealed in the Bible, not as we might want Him to be."[2]

Worship that is done publicly and privately is worship that celebrates who God says He is in the Bible. Let the Bible inform your worship. You cannot worship God as you want Him to be. You worship God for who the Bible says He is, for what your spirit knows to be true that's in line with His Word.

---

2. Donald S. Whitney, Spiritual Gifts for the Christian Life (Colorado Springs, CO: NavPress, 1991), 89.

Chapter Three

Loving the Community

D o you recognize churches or Christians based on their reputation?

I think it is natural and probably even healthy to do so. Jesus did this in the book of Revelation. Jesus knew the works of the churches mentioned in the book of Revelation. He either had good things to say or bad things to say to them based on their reputations. Sometimes, He had both good and bad things to say. In Revelation 2-3, Jesus says, "I know your works" to the church in Ephesus, Thyatira, Sardis, Philadelphia, and Laodicea.

Jesus not only knows the work of the church, He gave it its mission in Matthew 28.

> Go therefore and make disciples of all
> nations, baptizing them in the name of
> the Father and of the Son and of the
> Holy Spirit, teaching them to observe

> all that I have commanded you. And be-
> hold, I am with you always, to the end of
> the age. (Matthew 28:19-20.)

You, along with your church, are to go from the comfort and safety of your church building and make disciples of all nations. This is a call to the church, but also to the Christian. You don't get to sit back on the sideline and watch ministry. Get in the game of evangelism and discipleship. Reach your world for Jesus.

Luke records Jesus' last words to the church before He ascended.

> But you will receive power when the
> Holy Spirit has come upon you, and you
> will be my witnesses in Jerusalem and in
> all Judea and Samaria, and to the end of
> the earth (Acts 1:8.)

I am the Senior Pastor of White Plains Baptist Church, a Southern Baptist Church in Scottsville, Kentucky. As Southern Baptists, we take this call to go into the world and share the hope of Jesus seriously. Southern Baptist Churches financially contribute to the Cooperative Program. The Co-

operative Program is how White Plains funds and
supports outreach outside of what we do locally in
Scottsville.

Much of the financial support that goes to the
Cooperative Programs funds international missions
and missional efforts in North America. In our case,
there is a portion that stays in our state with the
Kentucky Baptist Convention. Much of that state
portion is devoted to state-wide evangelism efforts
and caring for orphans in Kentucky.

This is good. Our church does well by giving toward
the Cooperative Program, but this is not all we can
or should do. The Cooperative Program doesn't do
what we can most easily do, and that is, love the
community. Do you know what types of outreach
programs your church is part of? Are you actively
involved in praying and supporting those efforts?

Scottsville, Kentucky, is a small town in a section of
the United States known as the Bible Belt. There are
over 23,000 people who live within 10 miles of our
church building. There are over 30 churches in that
same area. Our little town has more churches than
it has restaurants and gas stations combined. Maybe
your church and town are about the same.

I often wonder about those 23,000 people who live near our church building. What do those 23,000 people think of church? What do they think of our church? Does our church have a reputation of love for the community, for them? I hope so. As the pastor, I hope there are a few things our church has a reputation for in the community. One of those things is love for the community.

What about your church? Regardless of how many people live near your church and how many other churches there are in your area, what do the people around your church think of church? What do they think of your church? Does your church have a reputation in the community? What is it?

Do you realize that most of the people who live within 10 miles of your church building don't go to any church? Even in the Bible belt, most of the people who live within 10 miles of your church building don't go to any church. They may claim Christianity or even claim a church as their home, but they haven't stepped foot regularly inside a church building in several years. This is your local mission field. This is largely why your church exists, to take the gospel to your friends, neighbors, and co-workers.

Loving the Community for the Sake of the Gospel

The church is the only Biblical organization that is tasked with taking the gospel to the community. I am thankful for businesses like Chick-fil-A and Hobby Lobby, but you can't expect businesses to drive gospel conversations in the community. I am thankful for groups like CRU (I met my wife at CRU) and the Navigators on the college campus and FCA on the local school campuses, but they aren't the church. They exist to support the gospel effort of the local church, not to replace it.

It is the church; it is you and your fellow church members who are to take the gospel to the community. This gospel effort is the foundation of the way you love the community. Look back at John 3:16 from the last chapter.

> For God so loved the world, that he gave his only Son, that whoever believes in him should not perish but have eternal life. (John 3:16.)

Think about this verse for a moment, especially considering the definition of love we discussed as we studied 1 Corinthians 13 earlier. God doesn't love the world in how many people in the world would want to define love. God doesn't just accept people as they are and leave them in their sinful condition.

Let me be clear, though, God does absolutely accept people as they are. But in His love for them, life change follows conversion.

God's love for you involves His working in your life to change you from what you were to what His ideal for you is. This goes for the community outside your church as much as it goes for you and those inside your church.

Who comes to Christ and remains the same? **No one**.

This is the model of gospel love you should have for the community. Lovingly welcome people and show hospitality to those outside the church regardless of their sin. As they come to understand God's love and desire for them, point them to turn from their sin just as you turn from your sin. It is a continual process for everyone.

Love the community by showing them Jesus, by telling them of Jesus, and by living like Jesus. Martin Luther said it this way,

> "Every Christian must become Christ to his neighbor." - Martin Luther

It is your duty to be Christ to the surrounding community. You cannot expect the community to come to church already Christ-like; you must go to the community to evangelize and disciple.

So what is evangelism? R.C. Sproul defines it below.

> "Evangelism, in its simplest definition, is "gospeling" or "making the gospel known." - R.C. Sproul[1]

Make the gospel known. But do it with finesse, keeping in mind the definition of love from 1 Corinthians 13. Don't become a noisy gong to your community.

---

1. R. C. Sproul, What is the Great Commission?, First Edition, The Crucial Questions Series (Orlando, FL: Reformation Trust, 2015), 10.

Are there some churches that are noisy gongs in your community? Sure, there are. Don't be one. Share the truth of the gospel in love so that the community hears the beauty of the gospel.

Loving the Community by Meeting Their Felt Needs

In sharing the gospel, you will definitely confront the sins of the community. Every community has idols. Some of those idols are national, but there are some that are also regional or local.

What local idols do you think you have in your community?

Have you ever considered why communities have idols?

Regardless of what the community idolizes, there are reasons people are drawn to worship things other than God.

Why?

What are those reasons?

Tim Keller says in his book, "Loving the City":

"Having entered a culture and challenged its idols, we should follow the apostle Paul in presenting Christ to our listeners as the ultimate source of what they have been seeking." – Tim Keller[2]

Defining Your Local Mission Field

Your friends, family, neighbors, and co-workers are searching for something. Everyone is searching for something. God has put that desire to seek after something greater than ourselves inside each one of us to direct us toward Him. But the community misses that and attempts to find hope, purpose, and joy in idols that are far from what God's desire is for them. Full disclosure, the church and those inside it do this as well. But it is not what God wants for any of us.

The community seeks idols because we feel the pain of sin. The community's desire to worship idols points to their need for the gospel.

---

2. Timothy Keller, et al., Love the City: Doing Balanced Gospel-Centered Ministry in Your City, Center Church (Grand Rapids, MI: Zondervan, 2016), 84.

Take the gospel to your community by meeting its felt needs. Go to the community on their terms. Love the community the way they will feel loved, for the sake of the gospel.

Some Felt Needs in the Community

Our church received some demographic data[3] about the surrounding community. Churches often use this type of data to help them understand the needs and ministry opportunities around them. Here are just a few things this report showed us:

(The first number is the percent of the local population who said the statement was important, the second number is the percentage of the total US population who said the statement was important. In the cases below, my community was more interested in them than those in the US.)

- Dealing with Teen/Child Problems - 26.3% / US 20.7%

- Dealing with Alcohol/Drug Abuse - 21.2% / US 16.7%

- Dealing with Problems in School - 19.1% / US

---

3. Ministry Area Profile 2021. Percept Group, Inc.

13.6%

- Dealing with Abusive Relationships - 14.6% / US 11.4%

This information probably isn't news to you. Your community may be very similar. There are other things on the report, but these are the largest felt needs in my community, and they are noticeably higher here than in the US as a whole. Our church should pay attention to this information as we seek to love the community by meeting its felt needs. As you and your church discover the felt needs of your community, use that information to meet the needs of those around you. Even if you don't have access to reports like this, you can get a sense of what your community needs by being involved in the community.

When you look at a report like this, and you know a community, what do you see? There is a real opportunity for ministry right here in Scottsville, Kentucky, isn't there? There are just as many needs in your community as well.

Remember, you and your church aren't alone. In a community like yours, your church doesn't have to tackle every need alone. Thankfully, there are some churches in my community, that are actively trying to love the community through the felt need to deal with alcohol and drug abuse. Your community probably has churches attempting to love the community through some of its felt needs. Perhaps your church has already identified some outreach strategies based on the felt needs of the community. Talk to your church to see how you can join their efforts to love the community.

As far as my church, we have used data from this report to help love the community. Things may change over time, but one way we are trying to love the surrounding community is by feeding all the high school sports teams at least once during their season. We hope that student-athletes in our community know that God loves them and that we, as a church, love them and are pulling for them. Many of us in my church were high school athletes, and we remember the joys and heartbreak that accompany competition. We want to insert the gospel and the church in that drama of life so that as kids deal with the highs and lows of sports; they know there is a church just down the road who loves them and will lovingly share the hope of Jesus with them when they may need it most. Our church building is within a mile of each school building in our county, so this way of showing love may not make sense for you. In our context, and given that we have many school teachers and administrators in our congregation, it is an effective way for us to show love to the community.

At the beginning of the school year, we recently expressed love to our school staff by giving them a prayer card and a coffee gift card. Based on the data above, we understand there are tremendous burdens placed on our school staff to care for and educate the children of our community.

Those who go into education have a love for kids that is needed for the students to thrive, but that love can quickly get exhausting. Did you know every problem sin causes in the community finds its way into the classroom? Schools see everything. They probably see more than most churches see. Teachers are on the front lines of dealing with the effects of sin.

In giving these prayer cards and coffee gift cards, our church desired to let our school staff know we love them and we are here to support them through prayer or any other way. The school system is a large employer in our community, and if our church can show gospel love to the school's staff, I trust God will bless that and use that effort to affect staff and student lives, along with the rest of the community, in ways that we may never know.

Our church is trying to love the community considering two of these felt needs in the report mentioned above; dealing with teen/child problems and problems in school.

This is becoming part of our reputation in the community. We want to be a church that loves the community by loving those in our schools, both staff and students.

This is not for the glory of White Plains. We are doing this for the glory of God. I don't know of any other churches in my area that are actively trying to love the community in the ways we are attempting. For the glory of God, we are trying to fill gaps in the collective church's local mission to the community.

What about you and your church? What can you do to show love to your community for the sake of the gospel? If your church isn't doing anything, talk to your pastor and see what simple steps you can begin taking as a church to love them well.

Spiritual Needs in the Community

There were some encouraging things from that earlier report that make ministry in our community meaningful. There are probably encouraging things like this in your community, as well.

People in my community value:

(The first number is the percent of the local population who said the statement was important, the second number is the percentage of the total US population who said the statement was important. In the cases below, my community was more interested in them than those in the US.)

- Finding a Good Church - 28% / US 15.2%

- Finding Spiritual Teaching - 22% / US 12.9 %[4]

One of the wonderful things about our community is there is still value in finding a wonderful church. It's almost twice as important to those in our community as opposed to the rest of the US. Finding good teaching is important, as well. This information encourages me to lead my church to be

---

4. Ministry Area Profile 2021. Percept Group, Inc.

a wonderful church in the community's eyes and to make sure I preach and teach from the Bible.

What do you think are some spiritual needs in your community? How can you and your church meet those spiritual needs?

Loving the Community Through a Strategic Approach

As I look at a report like this, I see a couple of things our church must do. We should continue to love those in our schools as a local ministry outreach and expand what we can do for the gospel in those areas. We must have an excellent reputation as a church with sound biblical teaching. God will surely bless our gospel efforts if we continue with this strategy.

What about you? Every community and church context is different. Spend time in prayer and evaluate your church's local mission field to develop a strategic approach to love the community for the sake of the gospel.

Chapter Four

Loving Other Christians

Should you love those in your church differently than you love those in the community? Jesus commanded you to love God and love others, so why distinguish between those in the community and those within the walls of your church?

> Let love be genuine. Abhor what is evil; hold fast to what is good. Love one another with brotherly affection. Outdo one another in showing honor. Do not be slothful in zeal, be fervent in spirit, serve the Lord. Rejoice in hope, be patient in tribulation, be constant in prayer. Contribute to the needs of the saints and seek to show hospitality.

> Bless those who persecute you; bless and do not curse them. Rejoice with those who rejoice, weep with those who

weep. Live in harmony with one another. Do not be haughty, but associate
with the lowly. Never be wise in your
own sight. Repay no one evil for evil, but
give thought to do what is honorable in
the sight of all. If possible, so far as it
depends on you, live peaceably with all.
Beloved, never avenge yourselves, but
leave it to the wrath of God, for it is
written, "Vengeance is mine, I will repay, says the Lord." To the contrary, "if
your enemy is hungry, feed him; if he is
thirsty, give him something to drink; for
by so doing you will heap burning coals
on his head." Do not be overcome by evil,
but overcome evil with good. (Romans
12:9-21.)

Loving Each Other is Good for You

Love other Christians. Loving each other is good
for you. You benefit from your love and good works
done toward other Christians.

"When Christians do grow in their love
for each other, for no other reason than

> because they are loved by Jesus Christ
> and love him in return, that growing
> love is an infallible sign of grace in their
> lives."—D. A. Carson.[1]

God is at work in you as you express your love
for each other. In the last chapter, we talked about
loving the community. In this chapter, we are talking about loving each other, specifically the other
Christians you go to church with. You should love
both. These are the neighbors who Jesus is talking
about in the Great Commandment.

> But when the Pharisees heard that he
> had silenced the Sadducees, they gath-
> ered together. And one of them, a
> lawyer, asked him a question to test him.
> "Teacher, which is the great command-
> ment in the Law?" And he said to him,
> "You shall love the Lord your God with
> all your heart and with all your soul
> and with all your mind. This is the great

---

1. D. A. Carson, Praying with Paul: A Call to Spiritual Reformation (Grand Rapids, MI: Baker Aca-
demic, 2014), 46.

and first commandment. And a second
is like it: You shall love your neighbor as
yourself. On these two commandments
depend all the Law and the Prophets."
(Matthew 22:34-40.)

You love the community and each other differently,
don't you? This is natural. You love the members
of your family differently than you love a stranger
across town? You still love both, but loving other
Christians differs from loving the community. Look
at 1 John 4:7.

Beloved, let us love one another, for
love is from God, and whoever loves has
been born of God and knows God. (1
John 4:7.)

When the Bible speaks of "one another", it speaks
the same way as I am when I say "each other." "One
another" means other Christians, especially those
you go to church with. The Bible says when you love
other Christians, you show you are a Christian.

As proof of your salvation, look at how you love
other Christians, not the ones who are like you, but
those who are the most difficult to love. Loving each

other is good for you because it shows you that you have been born of God and that you know God. It shows that you are following Jesus.

> "I am told that Christians do not love each other. I am very sorry if that be true, but I rather doubt it, for I suspect that those who do not love each other are not Christians."—Charles Spurgeon.

If you don't love other Christians, especially the ones in your church, you prove you may not be a Christian at all. Remember 1 John 4?

> No one has ever seen God; if we love one another, God abides in us and his love is perfected in us. (1 John 4:12.)

When we love each other, we make visible an invisible God. If we don't love each other, how can we see the unseen? If we don't love each other, how can the world see the unseen?

A Christian Who Doesn't Love Other Christians is Probably Not a Christian

Make sure you hear me when I say that; a Christian who doesn't love other Christians is probably not a Christian. Can you think of someone who claims to be a Christian but does not love other Christians? That person is in eternal danger.

Love is an important activity in the life of a Christian. The lack of love should be a serious wake-up call to those who claim to be Christian. John Stott helps us understand why.

> "We are to love each other, first because God is love, secondly because God loved us, and thirdly because, if we do love one another, God lives in us and his love is made complete in us."—John Stott[2]

Not loving is easy. To not love each other, nor anyone else, is natural. It is who you are outside of

2. John R. W. Stott, The Letters of John: An Introduction and Commentary, vol. 19, Tyndale New Testament Commentaries (Downers Grove, IL: InterVarsity Press, 1988), 165.

Christ. But when you encounter God's love for you, you understand God to be loving. He loves you, and as you love each other, you are imitating your God. This is good. It is right. It is Biblical. Let's look at the Gospel of John.

> A new commandment I give to you, that
> you love one another: just as I have loved
> you, you also are to love one another.
> (John 13:34.)

You are to love each other in the same way that Jesus loves you. So, how did Jesus love you? He gave His life for you.

The love of Jesus is sacrificial. Sacrifice for others in your church to love like Jesus.

When You Love Other Christians, You Become More Like Christ

As you love other Christians, you become more like Jesus. Loving each other is good for you. You are obedient to God as you love other Christians. Here's a list of all the commands in the New Testament to love each other. Read through these passages this week, and you will clearly see that you are to love other Christians.

Love God Verses

Deuteronomy 6:5; 11:1,11:13, 11:22; 13:3; 19:9; 30:6, 30:16, 30:20

Joshua 22:5; 23:11

Matthew 22:37

Mark 12:30

Luke 10:27

Love The Community Verses

Leviticus 19:18

Matthew 5:43; 5:44; 19:19; 22:39

Mark 12:31

Luke 6:27; 6:35

Romans 13:9

Galatians 5:14

James 2:8

Love Each Other Verses

John 13:34; 15:12; 15:17

Romans 13:8

1 Thessalonians 4:9

1 Peter 1:22

1 John 3:11; 3:23; 4:7; 4:11; 4:12

2 John 5

Loving Each Other is Good for the Church

While loving each other is good for you, it is also good for your church. You probably know the name John Wesley, right? He was an itinerant preacher. John Wesley would go from town to town to preach and set up churches. He founded the Methodist Church doing this. He warns us about a church that doesn't love each other.

> "Beware of schism, of making a rent in the Church of Christ. That inward dis-union, the members ceasing to have a reciprocal love 'one for another,' is the very root of all contention, and every outward separation."—John Wesley.

If you are in a church with visible disunity and vocal factions, you probably have a church without love. It's not a good place to be. The lack of love for each other is bad for the church. In fact, you should have an expectation that when you come to church, they will love you. With that expectation to be loved, they also expected you to love them. Paul says to make a friendly competition of it.

> Love one another with brotherly af-
> fection. Outdo one another in showing
> honor. (Romans 12:10.)

Have you ever played that "I love you more" game with your kids or spouse? Where you end up getting into a spirited debate over who loves who the most. Do that at church, at least until the debate gets heated.

Work hard to love each more than they love you. Outdo one another in showing love to those in your church. Keep it classy and don't get into arguments about it. Your church will be better for it, as you seek to show love to each other more and more.

Do you remember the definition I gave you for love in the first chapter of this book?

Love wants the best for someone else.

Thomas Aquinas was a Catholic priest in the 1200s, and he defines love similarly.

"To love is to will the good of another."
—Thomas Aquinas.

Aquinas was a philosopher, as well as a priest, and a theologian. When you love each other, you are willing their good. The church benefits when you love each other.

Do you realize that almost every other organization in the world is marred by division, ego, and hatred? The church isn't perfect, but when you strive to live out what you have been called to be and do, you stand apart from all the other organizations because you make the church a place where those inside can have genuine love for each other. The church stands out from the rest of the world when we love each other. This is only possible by the grace of God.

The Bible gives you much to consider in how you interact with other Christians. Here is a list of all the "one another" passages in the New Testament. Once you become a Christian, you don't have to wonder what you are to do. This list helps you to know how to interact with each other at church. Spend some time looking through the list this week and see how you can love others better around your church.

"One Another" Verses in the New Testament

Mark 9:50

John 13:14; 13:34; 13:35; 15:12; 15:17

Romans 12:10; 12:16; 13:8; 14:13; 15:7; 15:14; 16:16

1 Corinthians 11:33; 12:25; 16:20

2 Corinthians 13:12

Galatians 5:13; 5:15; 5:26; 6:2

Ephesians 4:2; 4:32; 5:19; 5:21

Philippians 2:3

Colossians 3:9; 3:13; 3:16

1 Thessalonians 3:12; 4:9; 4:18; 5:11

Hebrews 3:13; 10:24; 10:25

James 4:11; 5:9; 5:16

1 Peter 3:8; 4:8; 4:9; 4:10; 5:5; 5:14

1 John 3:11; 3:23; 4:7; 4:11; 4:12

2 John 5

Loving Each Other is Good for the Community

Loving each other is good for you, it's good for the church, and it is good for the community. We cannot separate our love for each other from the gospel. It is our love for each other that God uses to draw the world to the church. This is how the Gospel Coalition says it.

> "The church is distinguished by her gospel message, her sacred ordinances, her discipline, her great mission, and, above all, by her love for God, and by her members' love for one another and for the world."—The Gospel Coalition.

You Must Love Other Christians

John writes, "By this all people will know that you are my disciples, if you have love for one another. " (John 13:35.)

Love other Christians for the sake of the gospel. This type of love is uncommon. It is something you must work toward. Love each other to be obedient to God's desire for you, the good of each other, and for the sake of the community.

You proclaim the gospel as you love other Christians well. As you love other Christians, you love God. As you love other Christians, you proclaim the gospel to your church. Paul tells you to outdo each other in showing honor. Your love for other Christians and its amount for them is tied to your love for God and for the community.

Practice Loving Each Other

Are you loving other Christians well? Are you part of a loving church where you feel loved as much as you love others there? There are some in your church who probably need to be loved more or better. There are some who need you to go to them and begin the out-doing each other in friendly competition.

Would you attempt to go to them and introduce yourself this coming Sunday?

Here are three ways to practice loving other Christians.

Serve each other.

Most church volunteers don't serve for the recognition, but I think it is healthy for you to know how things get done in your church and by whom. Your church cannot do many of the things it does without volunteers. Are you serving in your church?

Most churches have members who don't serve. That is not uncommon, but it is not healthy, either. There are many ways to serve. Talk to a ministry leader or pastor at your church about how you can serve. That is one conversation they will be happy to have with you.

Pray for and with each other.

Prayer is something you can do anytime to show love for other Christians. How does your church share prayer requests? Are you aware of the prayer needs of your church? Do you pray regularly for the needs of other Christians in your church?

You should also get into the habit of praying with each other. I know for many, it's weird to pray out loud in front of someone else. But it is a great way for you to love other Christians. Are you part of a Bible study or class in your church where you can pray with the group? Is there a close Christian friend in your church that you can pray with regularly?

Fellowship with each other.

Spend time with each other. Get to know each other. Build each other up. Look around the worship center or sanctuary of your church this weekend and introduce yourself and get to know others there. Let them get to know you as you get to know them.

Love those in your church by serving them, praying for and with them, and fellowshipping with them.

Chapter Five

Bonus Chapter: Loving Kids Like Jesus

I spent many years as a student pastor. The first church I served in was during my college years. I was part of a team of college students pouring into the lives of teenagers in that church. I loved it, but they also gave me the responsibility to teach a Sunday School class of fifth and sixth graders. As I write this chapter, it is important to note that I currently have a sixth-grade daughter.

I remember those kids well. The class was called the 56ers. These class members quickly picked up on a quality I have always seemed to have. In His wisdom, God has given me a special ability to connect with kids by becoming a punching bag and/or a climbing toy for them. I still have this quality. If you ever attend the church I pastor and have a kid in the preschool or elementary age group, it is likely that they will punch me. They will probably do it right in front of you. It's okay. I am used to it and have matured since what I'm about to unfold in the next few paragraphs.

With this 56ers class, as I was teaching them one Sunday morning, the entire class climbed on me - at the same time. There might have been five or six kids in this class, but as they disregarded the lesson I was teaching and any personal space I thought I had, it felt like there were twenty to thirty kids.

Have you ever found yourself in a situation you didn't know how to get out of?

I was definitely in one of those situations. Those kids overwhelmed me. I became their jungle gym. I was immature, unsupported, alone, and overwhelmed.

So do you know what I did?

I left. I just walked out.

Somehow, God, in His mercy, gave me the strength to climb my way out of that pack of ravenous kids. I made it to the door, and I slipped out. I even left the building and remember looking at the sidewalk as I walked away. There were just a couple of minutes left before their parents were going to come and get them. I believe there was another teacher in the room with me, at least, I hope so.

If you were to find anyone from that church today, they wouldn't know what happened or even remember me. For all I know, the teacher that used to be in that class before me did the same thing and left them, but never came back.

As I think back to that time, I realized I abandoned, even for just a couple of minutes, the ministry God was leading me into. I couldn't articulate it to you that way then, but that's what I did.

Just to ease your mind, I have had over 20 years of successful student and kid's ministry history, and I have left no one since that 56ers class in the late 90s.

I love student ministry. I believe it is essential, but I see kids' ministry as being the most important stage of life ministry a church can undertake. Please don't misunderstand me, all stage of life ministries are important, but if a church misses the kids' ministry stage, she misses the most important stage of spiritual development and gospel decisions. Student ministry used to be that stage, but over the past 10 to 15 years, there has been a shift younger in stage of life ministries.

So in this bonus chapter, I want to look biblically at kids' ministry. You will see that Jesus loves kids.

But Jesus said, "Let the little children come to me and do not hinder them, for to such belongs the kingdom of heaven." (Matthew 19:14.)

Disciple Kids and Love Them Like Jesus

We are to disciple kids and love them like Jesus. How do we love them like Jesus? The church's ministry to kids, in my mind, is the most important stage of life ministry that she can undertake. If a church doesn't reach their kids and the kids of the community with the gospel, there won't be a student ministry, a young adult ministry, or even young families in the church. The death of the church will soon follow.

A church should not reach kids just to develop a feeder ministry for all the other ministries, but it never fails when a church reaches kids, the student ministry grows, the young adult ministry grows, and the church will have young families as part of the church family. A church must reach kids with the gospel because Jesus loves kids.

To love kids like Jesus, we must create moments and environments at home and at church that God uses to draw kids to Himself.

Jesus said, "Let the little children come to me and do not hinder them, for to such belongs the kingdom of heaven." (Matthew 19:14.) Jesus loves kids. You should love kids, too, if you are to follow in Jesus' footsteps. As a church creates moments and environments, the church must be careful in what they teach them.

Kids come to Jesus when people share the gospel with them.

This is the only way. Share the gospel with kids. Do this in your home and in your church building. Share the gospel with your kids. Especially, if you are a parent or grandparent.

Don't hinder kids with extra works. Share the truth of God's grace. The gospel alone is what God uses to save kids and adults alike. You must never add to the gospel to change someone's behavior before coming to God. God meets everyone right where they are. That includes kids. The gospel shows God loves kids even in their brokenness. He has made known the way for kids to be made right with Him, and He will use people like you to point kids to the gospel, and He will save some.

A role of Christian adults and teenagers is to help kids apply the gospel to their lives. It starts with understanding that all people are sinful and need a rescuer. The Christian life continues in the gospel as we learn how to apply the truth of God's grace to every aspect of our lives. As you attempt to grow in that knowledge, share that with your kids at home and in your church.

Why? Jesus says that the Kingdom of Heaven belongs to kids, too. In fact, Jesus holds up the faith of kids as something for you to strive for. There may be questions about why God would allow some stuff to happen that you will never fully understand. It might bother you that you don't understand. Kids, mostly, are okay with not always understanding. If you have been around a genuine faith of a child, you have seen their wonder and amazement at God and their strong faith in just accepting that God is other than us and we may not be able to explain everything.

As you consider helping kids apply the gospel to their lives, there are two primary places you do that. You do that at home and at church.

Disciple Kids at Home

Let me speak briefly about discipling kids at home. If you don't have kids at home, you can pray for those of us who do, because it is difficult. Let's look at Ephesians.

> Fathers, do not provoke your children to anger, but bring them up in the discipline and instruction of the Lord. (Ephesians 6:4.)

Parents, lovingly and patiently teach your kids Biblical truth and spiritual disciplines. There are several spiritual disciplines you can teach your kids. I mentioned Donald Whitney's book, "Spiritual Disciplines for the Christian Life," earlier in this book. It is a great resource, but there is another one that is geared to teaching your kids spiritual disciplines, "Habits of a Child's Heart: Raising Your Kids with the Spiritual Disciplines" by Valerie Hess.

Here are some topics covered in "Habits of a Child's Heart."[1]

- Meditation

- Prayer

- Fasting

- Studying

- Service

- Confession

- Worship

It might seem overwhelming to do all of these well with your kids, so I want to give you three ways to begin to practice these spiritual disciplines.

- Read the Bible to your kids and have them read it to you.

- Teach your kids to pray and allow them the opportunity to pray with you and the family.

- Serve with your kids at church.

---

1. Valerie E. Hess. Habits of a Child's Heart; Raising Your Kids with the Spiritual Disciplines. (Colorado Springs, CO: NavPress, 2014).

Matt Chandler has written a book called "Family Discipleship." I would recommend it to those who are interested in discipling your kids or grandkids. He makes family discipleship seem attainable by focusing on three things.

1. **CREATING TIME** - Creating intentional time built into the rhythm of the family's life to think about, talking about, and living out the gospel. (p. 70).

2. **CAPTURING MOMENTS** - Capturing and leveraging opportunities in everyday life for gospel-centered conversations. (p. 91).

3. **MARKING MILESTONES** - Marking and making occasions to celebrate and commemorate significant spiritual milestones of God's work in the family's life and child. (p. 109).[2]

In Deuteronomy, we read the following.

---

2. Matt Chandler, and Adam Griffin. Family Discipleship: Leading Your Home through Time, Moments, and Milestones. (Wheaton, IL:Crossway, 2020.)

And these words that I command you
today shall be on your heart. You shall
teach them diligently to your children,
and shall talk of them when you sit in
your house, and when you walk by the
way, and when you lie down, and when
you rise. (Deuteronomy 6:6-7.)

Discipling Kids at Home Must be Intentional and Centered on the Bible

Be intentional about teaching your kids. For many,
it is difficult to find the time to talk about spiritual matters at home. Careers and activities keep us
moving and bouncing around town. That's okay. I
am not saying to be less busy; I am saying to be intentional. Realize that teaching your kids about the
Bible is primarily a parent's and grandparent's responsibility. Deuteronomy tells us to use that time
running around to teach them. Turn the radio off
and talk about the Bible.

People do this with other things. For those who
have kids in sports or music, we help move them
along in their efforts, don't we? I love watching my
youngest daughter (the sixth grader), Ruby, practice

and play soccer. I have been her coach for her entire rec league career. Now that she is on the Middle School team, I get to watch her from the other side of the field. I love watching her out there and love our conversations on the way home. We talk about what I saw her do well and how she felt she did during practices or games. I celebrate with her the goals she scored and ask her about things she might struggle with on the soccer field.

I do this with my older daughter, Lily, too. She is gifted with the ability to sing and play the guitar. I love seeing her lead worship at church and in the student ministry. She is very talented with music and worship. We talk about what I see in her as she continues to pursue her passion for leading worship and she talks about what she felt she did well after leading. I celebrate with her as she stretches herself to grow, and I ask her about things she might struggle with musically.

To be honest with you, I know very little about soccer and I know even less about music and leading worship. But I have spent the effort to learn soccer and grew my understanding of music because I love my daughters.

Do this with spiritual matters, too. Even if you feel you don't know enough about the Bible or if you are afraid your kids might ask you a question you don't know how to answer. Be intentional and teach your kids the Bible.

Disciple Kids at Church

Whether or not there are kids at your home, there are kids at your church. You, along with the others in your church, should teach them.

> All your children shall be taught by the Lord, and great shall be the peace of your children. (Isaiah 54:13.)

The Gospel Brings Peace and Joy

John writes this in 3 John:

> I have no greater joy than to hear that my children are walking in the truth. (3 John 4.)

John is probably not speaking about young children
here, but of young believers in the faith. The point
holds, though. Those new to their faith bring joy
to leaders as they walk in the truth they have been
taught. When young believers apply the the Bible to
their lives, there is joy.

Churches must lovingly and intentionally disciple
kids. You and your church have a responsibility to
teach the Bible to the next generation. Do that lovingly and with intentionality.

Disciple Kids in the Community

Jesus loves kids. Teach Scripture to your kids at
home and at church, but don't forget about the
Great Commission. This applies to loving kids in the
community.

> And Jesus came and said to them, "All
> authority in heaven and on earth has
> been given to me. Go therefore and
> make disciples of all nations, baptizing
> them in the name of the Father and of
> the Son and of the Holy Spirit, teaching
> them to observe all that I have com-
> manded you. And behold, I am with you

always, to the end of the age." (Matthew 28:18-20.)

We are to make disciples of kids by sharing the gospel with them, baptizing them, and teaching them.

As a pastor of a church, I hope our kids will learn to love Jesus more and have a lot of fun learning about Him. So much so that they will encourage their parents to drive across town and pick up a friend or cousin and bring them to our building.

Teaching Kids Starts at Home, Continues at Church, and Goes to the Community

There are some kids who will never enter your church building. Strengthen your kids and their parents to be confident to take the gospel to the kids and families in your community. This is where your church's local outreach strategy develops. (See the chapter on Loving the Community.)

Do not overlook kids in your outreach. Jesus loves kids. Kids are part of "all nations." As you live in your community, be aware of the spiritual needs of the kids in your community.

> Train up a child in the way he should go;
> even when he is old he will not depart
> from it. (Proverbs 22:6.)

If there is "the way" a child should go, there are many ways he shouldn't go. The church must lead kids in the right way.

- Don't force them.

- Don't coerce them.

- Don't bribe them.

- Lead them in the right way.

- Love them.

- Train them in the way they should go.

As the church disciples the kids in the community, start with the gospel and then invite them with their families into the community and fellowship of the church.

Jesus said, "Let the little children come to me and do not hinder them, for to such belongs the kingdom of heaven;" how should we respond? I would say there are three things you can do.

- Pray

- Pursue

- Volunteer

About Author

With a passion for discipleship, Gary writes books and creates resources to help individuals and families follow Jesus. He joyfully serves as the Senior Pastor of White Plains Baptist Church in Scottsville, Kentucky. Gary is the founder of Discipleship Studio. He earned his Masters of Arts in Biblical and Theological Studies from Knox Theological Seminary in Fort Lauderdale, Florida.

Gary and his wife, Emily, live in Scottsville, Kentucky. They have two daughters, Lily and Ruby. Get more information about Gary at floydgarypierce.com

Also By Floyd Gary Pierce

Broken: The Problem of Sin

ISBN: 978-1965044032

Help your little one discover God's love and redemption.

"Because of Jesus, we aren't broken anymore."

With the help of their mother, the Bible, and a broken picture frame, two lovable sisters discover the reality of being broken by sin and the joy of God, making them new through the life and death of Jesus.

My Big Prayers: The Psalms, Part 1

ISBN: 978-1965044025

Help your little one develop a heart for God with this devotional prayer journal.

Available at https://discipleshipstudio.com

www.ingramcontent.com/pod-product-compliance
Lightning Source LLC
Chambersburg PA
CBHW010220140626
46545CB00014B/3138